MYSTERIES
OF THE ANCIENT WORLD

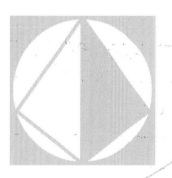

THE PYRAMIDS
STAR CHAMBERS
ROBERT G. BAUVAL

WEIDENFELD & NI
LONDON

Of all the monuments of the ancient world, none evokes more wonder and mystery than the Three Pyramids of Giza in Egypt. With their enigmatic companion the Great Sphinx, these strange 'man-made mountains'

The pyramids as seen by a 17th-century illustrator; engraving from Olfert Dapper Description of Africa *(Amsterdam, 1686).*

have attracted more scholars and crackpots alike than any other edifice on earth in the attempt to solve conclusively the riddle that they pose: Who built them? How were they built? When? And why?

Mystery in Stone

As if deliberately to bedevil the generations through the ages, the pyramids and Sphinx of Giza were left completely bare by their mysterious builders. No writings, no drawings and no arte-facts were ever found inside or outside the Giza pyramids. When the pyramids were opened in medieval times by the Arabs they were as empty as they are today. Strange corridors, galleries and chambers with smooth walls bereft of inscriptions are all you will see, and in each only a mysterious empty stone coffer, which modern Egyptologists have, perhaps too hastily, assumed to be coffins for dead kings. Austere and silent, the Three Pyramids and the Sphinx loom like gigantic question-marks on the desert sand, always taunting, always challenging those who gaze upon them.

Mysterious legends and myths abound about these structures. The most persistent is that the Giza Pyramids and the Sphinx are the legacy of a super-race of men, perhaps from the lost continent of Atlantis, who settled in Egypt after a great flood and there, at Giza, concealed all their knowledge and wisdom in a 'Hall of Records' under the bedrock. This century such ideas became widespread when America's famous 'Sleeping Prophet', Edgar Cayce, predicted that the fabled 'Hall of Records' of the Atlanteans would be discovered under the Sphinx or inside the Great Pyramid around the year 1998. Cayce died in 1945; today the Edgar Cayce Foundation, also known as the ARE (Association of Research and Enlightenment), has members all

Victorian tourists in 1880 about to climb the Great Pyramid from the south-west corner. Climbing is not allowed today.

over the world and since the early 1970s has sponsored several expeditions to Giza to search for the 'Hall of Records'. As we shall see later, recent findings suggest that Cayce might be right after all.

Egyptologists and archaeologists, of course, dismiss such ideas as pure fantasy. They see in them nothing but the obsessed dreams of myth-makers and psychics. To them the matter is classified and closed. There is no mystery here. The Three Pyramids of Giza are tombs for the pharaohs of the 4th Dynasty who ruled in about 2500 BC during an epoch known as the Old Kingdom. Recently, however, a group of new researchers has challenged such views with new scientific evidence. Using geology and astronomy as dating tools, they have shown that the Sphinx of Giza could be thousands of years *older* than Egyptologists think, and that, far from being tombs only, the Giza Pyramids may be part of a 'time capsule' put there by a highly advanced civilization that is yet to be discovered.

Could the myth of Atlantis be true?

Dynasty	Period	Years
1–2	Early Dynastic	3100–2686BC
3–6	Old Kingdom	2686–2181BC
7–10	First Intermediate	2181–2133BC
11–12	Middle Kingdom	2133–1786BC
13–17	Second Intermediate	1786–1567BC
18–20	New Kingdom	1567–1080BC
21–25	Late New Kingdom	1080–664BC
26	Sait	664–525BC
27–31	Late	525–332BC
	Ptolemaic	332–30BC
	Roman	30BC–AD642
	Arab	AD642–present

Chronological table of Egyptian civilization. The Pyramid Age took place in the Old Kingdom from the 3rd to the 6th Dynasties.

Pyramid Facts

There are some 92 pyramids in Egypt; this figure, however, is misleading. Many of these pyramids are simply small shrines built in later times and bear little or no resemblance to the scale and design of the Giza Pyramids. According to Egyptologists, the golden age of pyramid building in Egypt began in the 3rd Dynasty (*c*.2686 BC) and ended in the 6th Dynasty (*c*.2181 BC). During those few centuries over 25 'great' pyramids were built along a narrow strip of desert on the west side of the River Nile near the modern city of Cairo. Today this region is known as the Memphite Necropolis (necropolis means 'city of the dead' in Greek), and stretches from Dashour

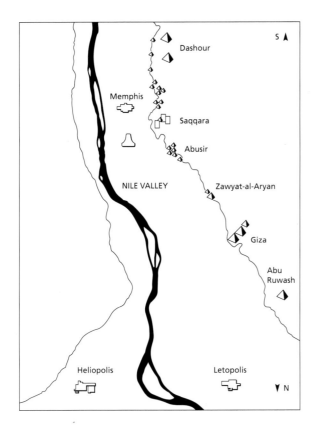

*M*ap of the Memphite Necropolis, showing the main pyramid fields of the Old Kingdom.

some 20 km from the modern city of Cairo, to Abu Ruwash, which lies 15 km to the north-west of the city. The Giza monuments are roughly at the centre of this 'land of the pyramids'.

The view among Egyptologists is that the Pyramid Age began when a man called Imhotep, a high priest and vizier of the pharaoh Zoser of the 3rd Dynasty (*c*.2681 BC), designed the famous Step Pyramid complex at Saqqara. This curious pyramid, which towers 60 m above ground level, along with

*T**he Step Pyramid is the oldest architectural project in history and was designed by the high priest and vizier Imhotep.***

boundary wall and temples, is the world's first architectural project. Although the Step Pyramid is a very large structure in its own right, it was to be dwarfed by the mighty pyramids of the great 4th Dynasty. The founder of this remarkable dynasty, the pharaoh Sneferu, dramatically increased the scale of construction and introduced the so-called 'true' pyramid design with slopes cased in smooth white limestone slabs.

Sneferu built two pyramids at Dashour, known today as the Red Pyramid and the Bent Pyramid. The casing slabs of the Red Pyramid have completely vanished – probably stripped off in the Middle Ages by the Arabs to build the mosques and palaces of Cairo. Without its white casing-slabs this pyramid glows with a reddish tint at sunrise and sunset, hence its modern name. The Bent Pyramid, which retains most of its original casing, is so named because it has a slope that changes halfway up the monument. Both pyramids are about 100 m tall and, altogether, contain more than 9 million tonnes of stone blocks.

Until recently the site of Dashour was closed to visitors because it was within an Egyptian military base. In October 1996, however, the Supreme Council of Antiquities acquired the site and it is now open to the general public. Only the Red Pyramid, however, can be entered. It has a most remarkable inner system with three enormous chambers having smooth walls and high corbelled ceilings bare of any inscriptions.

The son of Sneferu was Khufu, better known today as Cheops, a name

The Bent (or southern) Pyramid of Dashour. This is the only 4th Dynasty pyramid which has retained most of its smooth casing blocks.

given to him much later by the Greeks. Determined to outdo his father, Cheops commissioned an even more massive pyramid on a rocky platform overlooking the Nile Valley near the modern village of Giza, 10 km west of Cairo. Looming more than 140 m, like some huge tidal wave of stone, it is, in the words of one Arab historian, 'the mother of all pyramids'. Indeed, until the construction of the Eiffel Tower in Paris in 1889 and the Hoover Dam in Arizona in the 1930s, the Great Pyramid was the tallest and most massive

man-made edifice in the world. It contains no less than 6 million tonnes of stone, and its huge base, with sides that measure 230 m, is almost perfectly orientated to true north within 5 per cent of a single degree of arc.

It is calculated that the base of the Great Pyramid, which occupies an area of more than 4.5 hectares, is large enough to accommodate over 200 tennis courts. The superstructure of this amazing monument contains over 2.5 million blocks of stone each weighing an average of 2 tonnes. Yet some of the

*T**he Red
(or northern)
Pyramid of Dashour.
It is unique among
other 4th Dynasty
pyramids because
of its slope of only
43 degrees (others
have slopes of 51
degrees, or more).*

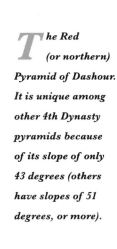

The Three Pyramids of Giza seen from the south.

*P*hotograph
of the
Great Pyramid
taken in 1890.

blocks used to construct the inner chambers high within the pyramid weigh over 40 tonnes each. To add to the mystery, many of these huge blocks were brought from Aswan, a region 1,000 km south of Giza. Such a feat of engineering and organization would task to the limit the most experienced modern construction companies. Needless to say, it is very hard to imagine how this project was achieved by people who supposedly had just emerged from the Stone Age with no knowledge of the pulley or even the wheel, and using only simple copper tools. Theories abound as to how the Great Pyramid was built, but the simple truth is that no one really knows for sure.

D etail of core masonry blocks of the Great Pyramid. Each block weighs an average of 2 tonnes.

*D*iorite statue of the Pharaoh Khafre,
builder of the Second Pyramid at
Giza (4th Dynasty). Cairo Museum.

*S*tatue of Menkaure flanked by two
goddesses; carved in green schist.
Cairo Museum.

The son of Cheops, Khafre, was known to the Greeks as Chephren. He,
too, built a huge pyramid at Giza almost as large and as perfect as his prede-
cessors'. He was followed by his son Menkaure, whom the Greeks called
Mycerinos. The latter raised the third and last 'great' pyramid at Giza. This
pyramid, however, is 65 m tall and thus less than half as tall as the other two.
Two other kings of the 4th Dynasty, Nebka and Djedefre, also planned pyramids near Giza, one at Zawyat Al Aryan to the south-east and the other at
Abu Ruwash to the north-east, but these were apparently never completed.
The 5th and 6th Dynasties built their pyramids at Abusir, some 10 km south

of Giza, and at Saqqara, which is a further 5 km to the south. These pyramids are much smaller than those of the 4th Dynasty; the quality of their
construction is shoddy and the accuracy of alignment inferior.

No mummies or funerary articles were ever found in any of the pyramids.
To add to this strange enigma, the great 4th Dynasty pyramids of Dashour
and Giza, as we have said earlier, do not contain inscriptions of any kind.
Yet, and in contrast to this stark nakedness, many of the 5th and 6th Dynasty
pyramids at Saqqara are full of hieroglyphic texts. These are known as the
Pyramid Texts. These and other later texts make it clear that the living king

*T*he Second
Pyramid of
Giza, built by the
pharaoh Khafre
(4th Dynasty),
viewed from the
top of the Great
Pyramid.

was regarded as the embodiment of the sun but that after his death his soul, called the *Ba*, would fly to the sky and become a star in a magical realm called the Duat. The Duat was the kingdom of Osiris, who, as the high god of resurrection and rebirth, was identified with the great constellation of Orion. According to these ancient texts, it was Osiris who had brought civilization to Egypt in a remote golden age known as Zep Tepi (the First Time). Horus, his only son, who was identified with the sun, was born from the womb of the great goddess Isis, herself identified with the bright star Sirius.

P *yramid Texts engraved inside the Pyramid of Unas (5th Dynasty).*

O *siris, god of resurrection and rebirth, flanked by the goddesses Isis and Nephthys. Papyrus of Ani. British Museum.*

During their lifetimes the pharaohs were believed to be the reincarnation of Horus, known in his solar form as Hor-Akhti, which means Horus of the Horizon. When a pharaoh died he was replaced by a new Horus, and his own soul became a star and joined Osiris in the heavenly Duat. As the Pyramid Texts proclaim:

Behold, Osiris has come as Orion . . . O King, the sky conceives you with Orion . . . you will regularly ascend with Orion from the eastern region of the sky . . . O King you are this great star, the companion of Orion, who traverses the sky with Orion, who sails in the Duat with Osiris. . . [Pyramid Texts, lines 820 and 882]

There can be little doubt, therefore, that the pyramids were regarded as the agency through which the souls of the departed kings could find their way to the stars of Orion in the Duat. A major clue supporting this idea is, of course, the astronomical alignment of the pyramids, which could only have been achieved by

stellar sightings. Another clue is the name 'Rostau', which was given to the Giza complex by the ancient Egyptians, and means 'the tunnel [or shaft] that leads to the Duat'.

There is also the fact that many of the pyramids were given star names. For example, two 4th Dynasty pyramids – at Zawyat Al Aryan and at Abu Ruwash – were called 'the pharaoh Nebka is a star' and 'the pharaoh Djedefre is a star in the Duat'. In the Pyramid Texts there is a pertinent passage which identifies the king with his pyramid and both, in turn, are identified with Osiris/Orion:

> *O Horus, this king is Osiris, this pyramid of the king is Osiris, this construction of his is Osiris . . .* [Pyramid Texts, line 1657]

This has lead some researchers to conclude that the pyramid builders saw the pyramids not as tombs but as 'stargates' to enter another cosmic dimension in Orion.

*T*he Three Pyramids of Giza (above); note the offset of the Third (smaller) Pyramid. The three 'Belt' stars in the constellation of Orion (right) are in the same formation

*T*he god Osiris flanked by his sister and wife Isis and his son Horus.

*The Opening
of the
Mouth ceremony,
part of the great
'cosmic' rituals
performed on the
mummy of the
dead king.
Papyrus of Ani.
British Museum.*

Gateway to the Stars

Inside the Great Pyramid are to be found two large chambers known as the King's Chamber and the Queen's Chamber. From each of these chambers emanate two narrow shafts, one directed to the south and the other directed to the north. The shafts are 20 x 20 cm across and slope upwards into the solid core of the pyramid. At first they were thought to be for ventilating the chambers, but recently it has been discovered that the shafts of the Queen's Chamber were closed at both ends, making such a function redundant.

In 1963 a team of researchers discovered that the shafts of the Great Pyra-

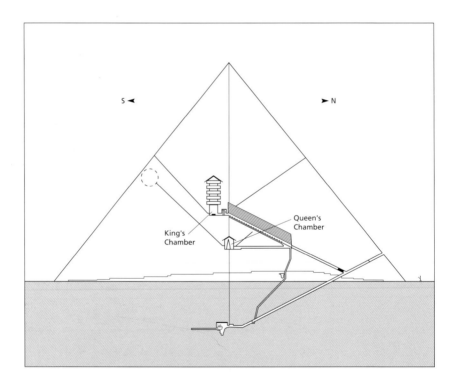

*S*outh–north (meridian) cross-section of the Great Pyramid showing the alignments of the four 'astronomical' shafts emanating from the chambers.

mid were astronomically aligned. Those going north were aimed at the circumpolar stars, and those going south towards the three stars in Orion's Belt (Osiris) as well as the bright star Sirius (Isis). Because these were the main stars of the Duat region which the souls of dead kings were supposed to inhabit, it was concluded that the Three Giza Pyramids were somehow imagined to have a direct connection with these special stars.

In 1984 a new theory was proposed by myself (developed in 1994 in *The Orion Mystery*). This theory shows how the pattern formed by the Three Great Pyramids and their relative position to the Nile mirrors the pattern formed by the three bright stars of Orion's Belt and their relative position to the Milky Way, the latter considered to be the 'Celestial Nile' by the ancient Egyptians. The giveaway was the offset of the third and smaller pyramid from the general layout plan. This was mimicked precisely by the similar position of the third and smaller (dimmer) star in Orion's Belt.

What the star/pyramid correlation also showed, however, was that the ground-to-sky patterns matched only in 10,500 BC. The position of the stars appears to change slowly over time, due to a phenomenon known as the precession of the equinoxes, which is caused by a slow, wobble-like motion of the axis of the earth over period of 25,920 years. Over such immense period of time the stars of Orion's Belt, for example, would appear to swing up and down like a huge pendulum. There is another effect of precession that is observed along the path of the sun across the 12 constellations of the zodiac; these, like the figures on a carousel wheel, appear to pass in front of a fixed point in the sky called the vernal point – the place the sun occupies during the spring equinox. The passing of a zodiacal constellation over the vernal point denotes an astrological 'age' which last some 2,160 years (12 x 2,160 = 25,920). The sun, of course, does not rise at the same place on the eastern horizon throughout the year. In midsummer it rises to the far north of due east, and in midwinter it rises to the far south of due east. It is only at the

Direct overhead aerial photograph of the Giza Pyramids. Note offset of the (topmost and smaller) Third Pyramid from the diagonal alignment of the other two larger pyramids.

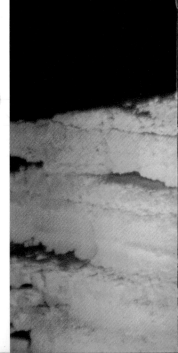

equinoxes (21 March and 21 September) that the sun rises due east.

The Great Sphinx of Giza was deliberately made to gaze due east, and thus can be said to be a marker of the equinoxes and, in astrological terms, the marker of an 'age'. But which age?

Since the birth of Jesus it has been the zodiac constellation of Pisces which contained the vernal point and rises due east on the day of the spring equinox. Soon it will be the constellation of Aquarius, marking the new Aquarian Age. At the epoch of 2500 BC, when the Sphinx is supposed to have been built, it was the Age of Taurus. Yet the Sphinx is carved in the shape of a lion, not a bull. We have to go back in time to 10,500 BC for the vernal point to be in the zodiac constellation of Leo. At this epoch the Great Sphinx would have gazed at its own image in the sky. The ancients called the Great Sphinx 'Horus in the Horizon of Giza'. We have seen how the solar image of the living pharaoh was also called 'Horus of the Horizon'. Several inscriptions found near the Sphinx dating to later periods confirm that the ancient Egyptians regarded the Sphinx of Giza, the ancient Rostau, as being the 'splendid place of the First Time'. These inscriptions also

*T*he Great Sphinx of Giza, known by the ancients as 'Horus in the Horizon'.

*The Giza
Necropolis
illuminated by
the sound and
light show.*

The moment of sunrise due east on the vernal (spring) equinox is 10,500 BC in conjunction with the passage of Orion's Belt due south at the meridian. Sphinx and pyramids appear to 'work' together an an architectural representation of this unique celestial conjunction.

speak of Osiris as Lord of Rostau, and how he had brought civilization to
Egypt in the First Time.

Computer simulation of the ancient skies show that the beginning (or First
Time) of the current precessional cycle of Orion occurred in 10,500 BC. The
computer also shows that on the day of the spring equinox in 10,500 BC Leo
would have been in direct alignment with the Great Sphinx at the exact time
the stars of Orion's Belt aligned with the Three Great Pyramids. It must be
noted, too, that the next time such a perfect sky-to-ground conjunction will
occur is in about AD 2100.

Could the Giza monuments, with their almost perfect astronomical alignments and correlation to Orion's Belt and Leo be a deliberate time marker
for the First Time, the pharaonic genesis? Is it possible that the mysterious
ancient builders use their sophisticated knowledge of astronomy to conceal a
map, not made from papyrus, which could easily be lost, but a map cleverly
drawn, as it were, on the billboard of the ancient sky in c.10,500 BC?

Today, with computer simulation, we can actually reconstruct this 'map'.
Oddly, the vernal point in 10,500 BC, and thus the spot marking 'X' on this
sky map, is directly under the rump of the celestial lion, the constellation of
Leo. For many years Egyptologists have known that a tunnel leads from the
rump of the Great Sphinx deep into an unknown location under the
bedrock. Recently an American team, lead by the Egyptologist John
Anthony West, using high-tech radar and sensing equipment have detected
several large cavities under the Sphinx, one of which lies near this tunnel.
The Egyptian authorities, however, deny there is anything in there and have
stopped all further exploration. Oddly, John Anthony West and his team also
discovered that the erosion and weathering of the Sphinx and its enclosure
would fix its age to around 10,500 BC.

In March 1993 the German robotics engineer, Rudolf Gantenbrink,
explored the mysterious narrow shafts of the Queen's Chamber in the Great

Pyramid and discovered at the end of the southern shaft a small stone door with two copper handles. The Egyptian authorities, here too, have stopped all further explorations of the shafts. Mounting media and public interest is pressurizing the Egyptians to act.

What, if anything, will be found in these secret chambers? Will they contain, as Edgar Cayce predicted, the records of a lost civilization?

Could the myth of Atlantis be true? Only time will tell.

The Great Sphinx and the Pyramids of Giza. Could the Sphinx be guarding a secret chamber under the bedrock?

PHOTOGRAPHIC ACKNOWLEDGEMENTS
Cover Robert Bauval [RB]; pages 2–3, 5, 8 Archiv
für Kunst und Geschichte London [AKG];
pp. 10–11, 12–13 RB; pp. 14, 16 AKG;
pp .17,18tl, 18–19, 20–21, 22, 23 RB; p. 24 AKG;
pp. 25br, 25bl, 26–7, 30–31, 32–3, 34–5 RB;
p. 38–9 E.T. Archive.

First published in Great Britain 1997
by George Weidenfeld and Nicolson Ltd
The Orion Publishing Group
5 Upper St Martin's Lane
London WC2H 9EA

Text copyright © Robert G. Bauval, 1997
The moral right of the author has been asserted
Design and layout copyright © George Weidenfeld
and Nicolson Ltd, 1997

A CIP catalogue record for this book is available
from the British Library
ISBN 0 297 823132

Picture Research: Joanne King

Design: Harry Green

Typeset in Baskerville